C000110123

24th November .

Winston Churchill

A Cherrytree Book

Designed and produced by
A S Publishing

First published 1988
by Cherrytree Press Ltd
a subsidiary of
The Chivers Company Ltd
Windsor Bridge Road
Bath, Avon BA2 3AX

British Library Cataloguing in Publication Data

Williams, Brian
    Winston Churchill. – (Children of history)
    1. Great Britain. Churchill, Winston S.
    (Winston Spencer)
    I. Title   II. Series
    941.082′092′4

    ISBN 0-7451-5002-0

Printed in Italy by New Interlitho, Milan

CHILDREN OF HISTORY

Winston Churchill

By Brian Williams · *Illustrated by* Martin Salisbury

CHERRYTREE BOOKS

The Young Churchill

Winston Churchill was called 'the greatest Englishman of the century'. When he died, in 1965, monarchs and presidents mourned the passing of a leader whose place in history was assured. During a long and adventurous life, Winston Churchill had for a time held in his hands the future not just of his own country but of the whole world.

Yet, as a boy, he had disappointed his parents, struggled with his schoolwork and constantly feared that he would fail to live up to the high standards expected of him.

An Aristocratic Family

Winston Leonard Spencer Churchill was born on 30 November 1874, the son of Lord Randolph Churchill. His mother was Jennie Jerome, an American from a wealthy family. Winston's birthplace was Blenheim Palace, a vast building near Woodstock in Oxfordshire. Blenheim had been built not for a monarch, but for a soldier named John Churchill, first Duke of Marlborough. Marlborough had defeated the French at Blenheim, Ramillies, Oudenarde and Malplaquet; Blenheim Palace was his reward.

Young Winston Arrives Unexpectedly

Randolph Churchill was born in 1849, the younger son of the seventh Duke of Marlborough. By the time his son Winston was born, Randolph was the newly-elected Member of Parliament for Woodstock; ambitious and clever, but also hot-headed. He was not a rich man (being a younger son, he would not inherit the dukedom).

The up-and-coming Randolph's beautiful, lively young wife Jennie was the daughter of Leonard Jerome, a New York financier. The couple had met at a society yachting

Winston's most famous ancestor was John Churchill, Duke of Marlborough (1650-1722). The duke was one of England's greatest soldiers. Blenheim Palace, where Winston was born, had been a gift to the duke from Queen Anne.

party at Cowes in 1873 and were married soon afterwards. Lord and Lady Churchill made a handsome couple in fashionable London society.

Lady Churchill was visiting Blenheim from her London home when her first child was born. Nothing was ready for the baby, so Winston was dressed in clothing borrowed from the wife of the local lawyer.

Today visitors from many countries come to admire Blenheim Palace and among all its treasures, the small room where Winston Churchill was born has a special place. For here began a remarkable story. The young Churchill grew to be a soldier, writer, politician and world statesman. As prime minister, he was to lead Britain during World War II in the fight against Adolf Hitler's Nazi Germany. In those dark days, Churchill's courage and determination were to inspire people all over the world.

THE FAMILY PALACE
The Duke of Marlborough's palace was named after a village on the River Danube: Blindheim, or Blenheim. There on 13 August 1704 his army won a great victory against the French and Bavarians.

Blenheim Palace was designed by the architect Sir John Vanbrugh. The buildings and courts cover seven acres (almost three hectares). Marlborough himself is buried there.

5

Winston, aged 2½, with his parents. Later, he wrote that his mother 'seemed to me a fairy princess'. Lord and Lady Churchill were a glamorous couple. Unfortunately, their busy lives left little time to spend with their children.

At Home in Ireland

In 1877 Lord Randolph took his family to live in Ireland, where his father, the Duke of Marlborough, had been appointed viceroy. In Ireland, then ruled by Britain, there was discontent and talk of 'Home Rule', or independence. Lord Randolph met the Irish leader Charles Stewart Parnell and became interested in the problems of the country.

A Second Mother

For Winston, only three years old, life in Ireland was happy and untroubled. His nanny, Elizabeth Anne Everest, was a second mother to him. He called her 'Woomany', and together they went for walks in Dublin's Phoenix Park to see the soldiers. At home, on the nursery floor, Winston loved to parade his own prized army. Collecting toy soldiers became a favourite hobby and eventually he had more than a thousand of these miniature models.

In February 1880 Winston's brother Jack was born, while he himself faced a new challenge: education. A governess was hired to carry on the start made by Mrs Everest, who had taught Winston the alphabet. When he saw the governess, Winston ran and hid in the garden. He especially hated maths. 'We descended into a dismal bog called sums', he later wrote. 'When I had mastered one sum, another came forward.'

The family's stay in Ireland ended soon afterwards, as a general election brought about a change of government. The Duke of Marlborough was no longer viceroy, and the Churchills returned to London. Lord Randolph was eager to pick up the threads of his political career.

The Churchills' nanny, Mrs Everest, became a second mother to Winston and Jack. She presided over the nursery, where Winston set out his model army on the floor. Today, his toy soldiers are displayed at Blenheim.

'He has no ambition . . .'

At the age of seven, Winston was sent to school. He had to leave his London home and live during term time at St George's School in Ascot. The school prepared boys for entrance to the great English public schools, such as Eton and Harrow. But St George's was not a good school. The teachers were grim figures in black caps and gowns. The boys were frequently beaten, and the food was poor. Winston was always hungry; his school report for 1884 contained the complaint that he was rather greedy at meals.

There were other complaints from the teachers at St George's. Winston was a beginner in most subjects. He did his best to master mathematics, French, history, geography, writing and spelling, and scripture. He tried hard, but it all seemed so difficult after the comfort of the nursery.

A Troublesome Boy

Winston did not behave very well, and the headmaster complained that he was 'always in some scrape or other'. On one famous occasion Winston is said to have seized the headmaster's straw hat from its hook and kicked it to pieces, after being flogged for stealing sugar from the pantry. Later the headmaster reported an improvement, though Winston's general conduct was 'still troublesome'. Worst of all, 'he has no ambition'.

Glad to Escape

However unhappy he may have been, Winston hid his feelings from his parents. He looked forward eagerly to the holidays, when he could escape to enjoy himself at Blenheim with Jack and their cousin 'Sunny' (who would one day be the ninth Duke of Marlborough).

Winston carried on a running feud with his school headmaster, Mr Sneyd-Kinnersley. After he had left St George's School, Winston was remembered as a boy 'whose naughtiness appeared to have surpassed anything'. Doubtless he was not as bad as all that, but he was frequently in trouble and up before the headmaster for a beating.

A New School

At the end of the summer term of 1884, Lord and Lady Churchill took Winston away from St George's. He had been unwell and a change of air was thought necessary. It is also possible that Mrs Everest had reported the scars left by Winston's beatings at school. With relief, Winston learned that he was to go to a new school, beside the sea, at Hove in Sussex. There was good news too for Lord Randolph. He had hopes of becoming secretary of state for India, should the Conservative party win the next election, and so he took a trip to India to see the country. Winston knew that his father was becoming an important man.

To Brighton

Winston's new school was run by two elderly sisters, Kate and Charlotte Thompson. He was much happier in Brighton; the school was smaller and more friendly, and both Miss Thompsons were kindly teachers. Winston's studies improved. He particularly enjoyed learning poetry by heart, and wrote to tell his mother how he also liked French, history and above all riding and swimming.

In her letters, Lady Churchill told him of her life in London and of his father's trip to India. Winston found that his parents were famous, even among his schoolfellows.

For several days during his illness with pneumonia Winston's life hung in the balance. The family doctor gave up his work in London to attend the young patient, and Lord and Lady Churchill hastened to Brighton to see their son. They waited anxiously until the doctor reported that the crisis was past.

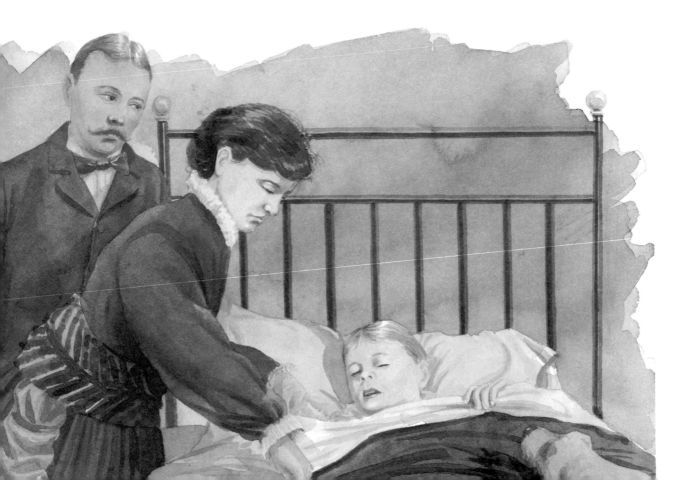

For much of his schooldays, letters were the closest link he had with his parents, for they seldom visited him. Most pupils at a boarding school could expect regular visits from their parents, especially for school concerts, plays and sports days. Lord and Lady Churchill rarely had time for such visits, and during the school holidays Winston and his brother Jack spent much of their time with Mrs Everest or with a governess. They looked forward eagerly to seeing their parents again, especially when the governess proved to be, in Winston's words, 'very unkind, so strict and stiff'.

A Dangerous Illness

In March 1886 Winston became seriously ill with pneumonia. Before the invention of antibiotic drugs, this disease was often fatal and for some time the boy's life was in danger. Lord and Lady Churchill hastened to his bedside. Fortunately, he recovered. The disease had attacked his lungs, but without lasting damage – as his later adventures and speech-making were to prove.

While he convalesced after the illness, Winston enjoyed working on his stamp album. His father had sent him some fine Indian stamps, and as Winston turned the pages of his collection, he began to realise just how large the British empire had grown.

Triumph and Disaster for Lord Randolph

Winston took a keen interest in politics, and in his father's career. In July 1886, Mr Gladstone's Liberal government was defeated in an election. The Conservatives swept into power, and Lord Randolph was appointed chancellor of the exchequer. It was the summit of Randolph's career. Still only 37, he was spoken of as a future prime minister. Sadly, within months, triumph had turned to disaster.

STAMPS OF EMPIRE
Winston's stamp album contained stamps from many distant lands. Many bore the head of Queen Victoria, showing that each territory was a member of the enormous empire. So vast was the British empire that children were taught that the sun never set upon it – meaning that at any hour, day or night, it was daytime in some part of the empire. Winston longed to see some of the countries whose stamps he had collected.

11

At the time of the jubilee the British empire was reaching the peak of its power. When young Winston looked at his school atlas, he saw almost a third of the world coloured red – indicating territory within the British empire.

From his window Winston looked out on the streets crowded with people celebrating Queen Victoria's long reign. Everywhere there were banners reading Vivat Regina! Long Live the Queen! He was determined to see the jubilee procession in London.

Randolph quarrelled with his colleagues over government finances and resigned as chancellor. He expected to be recalled, but the call never came. He would never rise so high again.

Enjoying the Golden Jubilee

The collapse of his father's political hopes did not lessen Winston's enjoyment of his last four terms at school in Brighton, though it cast a gloom over the whole Churchill family. Winston was more concerned with playing football and cricket, and learning his part as Robin Hood in the school play.

The summer of 1887 brought even greater excitement, not just in Brighton but throughout Britain and the empire. Queen Victoria was celebrating her golden jubilee. She had reigned for 50 years. In every village and town there were parades and ceremonies to mark the event.

Winston Gets His Way

Winston begged to be allowed to visit London to watch the jubilee procession in June. He wrote to his mother asking her to obtain permission for him to take time off school. He even drafted a letter for her to send to his teachers. Among the attractions he hoped to see was the famous Buffalo Bill, who had come from America with his Wild West Show.

In the end, he got his way. His mother wrote to Miss Thompson, she consented, and Winston went to join the family in London for the jubilee. He returned to school, content, and full of apologies for not behaving better while at home. He also asked for more pocket money, explaining that he was 'absolutely bankrupt'. No doubt the fun of the jubilee had been a little more expensive than he had bargained for.

Harrow

During the summer of 1887 Winston's parents considered the matter of his next school. Lord Randolph, and six previous generations of Churchills, had gone to Eton. However, Winston was enrolled at Harrow, Eton's great rival. Harrow School, situated on a hill, was thought to be more healthy than Eton, which lay in the damp Thames valley. The young new headmaster, the Reverend James Welldon, promised to keep a friendly eye on Winston, whose health still gave some cause for concern.

A Blank Page

Winston worked hard to prepare for the entrance examinations to Harrow. The subject that most perplexed him was Latin. When he saw the examination paper, his heart sank. He wrote his name at the top of the page. He wrote the number of the question: 1. After some thought, he added brackets: (1). Thereafter, he could think of nothing else to write and sat for two hours 'gazing at this sad spectacle'.

Mr Welldon evidently saw more in his new pupil than a blank Latin paper. Winston passed the exam, and in April 1888 he started as a new boy at Harrow.

More Pocket Money

Harrow schoolboys, wearing long trousers, jackets and top hats, were a familiar sight in the small town. The boys lived in houses, under the care of a housemaster. They came from the wealthiest families in the land, but pocket money was often a problem. Soon Winston was writing home to beg for more, to pay for the things he needed. He required food too (a chicken, three pots of jam and a plum cake, for example) to entertain his new friends.

YOUR NAME, BOY? Winston's family name, in full, was Spencer Churchill. At Harrow, this meant he appeared at the bottom of the alphabetical list of new boys, under 'S'. Winston wanted to stand higher in the list, under 'C', and wrote to Lord Randolph complaining that, as he always wrote his name 'Winston S. Churchill', this was how he ought to be listed. However, he remained Spencer Churchill on the school register.

The day before his prize-winning recitation of Macaulay's *Lays of Ancient Rome*, Winston discovered he had to learn an extra 200 lines – making 1200 lines in all. Fortunately, the task of memorizing the stirring verses came easily to him. He practised before the performance in the Speech Room at Harrow, adding some theatrical gestures to enliven the story.

The Young Orator

Winston was placed in the lowest class, but quickly found a way to make his mark. He had an excellent memory for poetry, and at the age of 13 won a prize for reciting Lord Macaulay's poem *Lays of Ancient Rome*. But despite this success, he ended his first term at the bottom of the class. Although his housemaster found him 'a remarkable boy in many ways', he also complained of Winston's 'phenomenal slovenliness' – late for school, losing books, forgetful, in fact 'regular in his irregularity'. It was not a very promising beginning.

. . . I Am Working Very Hard

Winston was to spend the next four and a half years at Harrow. Some subjects, such as Latin, he found difficult. Others, including English essay-writing, came easily to him. He formed a useful partnership with another boy, who could translate Latin very well. His friend translated Winston's work into English, and Winston memorized the translation. In return, Winston wrote essays for his friend, dictating them out loud while the other boy wrote in longhand. This arrangement worked splendidly until one particularly good essay attracted praise from the headmaster himself. He sent for the 'author' in order to discuss the

Although he was small, Winston was a pugnacious fighter. Fencing, he thought, was a useful sport to learn; it should help his military career. He practised hard in the school gymnasium and became school champion. He went on to become Public Schools Champion for 1892, only the second Harrow boy to achieve this distinction.

essay with him, and was rather surprised to find that he did not seem to know why he had written what he had.

Fencing and Field Days

Winston had set his heart on joining the army, and in 1889 when he was 14 he joined the army class at Harrow. Because he was not very good at maths, his teachers decided he had better try for Sandhurst (the Royal Military College that trained infantry and cavalry officers) rather than Woolwich (the college that took the more 'scientifically-minded' artillery and engineer cadets).

Winston worked hard at his schoolwork, intent on showing his parents that he could pass the examination. He joined the school's rifle corps and became a good shot. He also took up fencing. This became his favourite school sport, and by the age of 17 he was the fencing champion of Harrow. He also much enjoyed the field days, on which the Harrow rifle corps fought mock battles against rival schools. Winston drew sketch maps showing the positions of the opposing forces and sent them to his mother, with letters explaining how the two 'armies' had attacked and counter-attacked.

Summer holidays were often spent at the seaside, but with Mrs Everest, not with his parents. Once the Churchill boys stayed in a cottage on the Isle of Wight with Mrs Everest's sister, whose husband was a warder at the nearby prison. Lord and Lady Churchill remained loving but distant: it was not until Winston had been at Harrow for 18 months that Lord Randolph, at the headmaster's suggestion, came to see the school.

Early in 1891 Winston learned the good news that he had passed the preliminary examination for Sandhurst. But ahead lay the entrance exam itself.

Reluctantly, Winston gave up his holiday to spend some time in France, improving his French. Crossing the Channel to Dieppe in December 1891, he grumbled about everything. However, when he reached Versailles, he found his hosts welcoming, and he cheered up. In later life, he came to love both France and the French people.

Packed off to France

As his schooldays neared their end, Winston's work again seemed to falter. Mr Welldon, the headmaster, remained optimistic, and Winston did not appear to worry unduly either. He enjoyed holidays at the new family home in the country near Newmarket, where he and Jack built an impressive fort known as the Den. He went to London for the visit of the German Emperor in July 1891, saw fireworks and a parade of fire engines, and had the added pleasure of seeing Harrow beat their old rivals Eton at cricket.

Lord Randolph was away on a trip to South Africa; both his fortunes and his health were declining. Lady Churchill and Mr Welldon decided Winston would benefit from a foreign trip, too. He was packed off to France, to stay with a French family in Versailles. Winston protested: 'I beg and pray that you will not send me to a vile, nasty, fusty, beastly French family'. But he went anyway, and enjoyed it, because there were horses to ride and model soldiers to buy.

Two Failures, One Narrow Escape

Twice Winston took, and failed, the dreaded Sandhurst entrance examination. It was arranged that he should leave Harrow, and take private lessons to 'cram' for the exam. However, his arrival in London was delayed by an accident that might have proved fatal.

In January 1893 Winston was holidaying with an aunt near Bournemouth. While playing on the cliffs with his brother and cousin, he found himself 'trapped' by them on a bridge. Recklessly, he leaped off, hoping to slide down the fir trees to safety. He fell almost 10 metres, lay unconscious for three days, and was not well enough to resume his studies for almost two months.

Sandhurst

At his third attempt, Winston passed the Sandhurst entrance examination. However, his marks were not high enough to win an infantry cadetship; he was destined for the cavalry. Winston's father did not share in the general relief at his son's success. He wrote Winston a cross letter, rebuking him for 'slovenly, happy-go-lucky' work, and pointing out that the additional expense of maintaining a cavalry cadet would be a serious burden on the family finances.

In fact, Winston did join as an infantry cadet, when a place became vacant, and in September 1893 he began his new life at Sandhurst. His father's complaints rather soured his enjoyment of his first terms there, and he received little response to his requests for things he felt he needed – such as the money to buy a horse.

Lord Randolph, though Winston did not yet realise it, was seriously ill, and had not much more than a year to live. His friends were saddened at his decline; he was but a shadow of the dynamic figure he had once been.

I Am Very Contented . . .

Winston loved Sandhurst. Even the strict discipline did not lessen his delight in army life. On becoming a cadet, he was measured. His height was modest, only 1.7 metres, and his slim build aroused some concern. He was told to exercise. He hired horses from a nearby stables, for he loved riding and wrote that 'no hour of life is lost that is spent in the saddle'.

At home, though, Lord Randolph's money problems became even more acute. To his horror, Winston learned that Mrs Everest had been told to find a new place, in order

Winston loved horses. With his fellow cadets, he was taught to ride in the army fashion, and finished second in the Sandhurst riding competition. He and his friends organized point-to-point races and a cross-country steeplechase. He was determined to become not a foot-soldier, but a cavalry man.

to reduce the Churchills' household expenses. He thought her treatment 'cruel and rather mean', and continued to keep in touch with her.

He further incurred his father's displeasure by losing a pocket watch given to him by Lord Randolph. The watch fell into a pond, and to recover it Winston borrowed 23 soldiers and a fire engine to drain the pond dry. The watch was found, but had to be sent to the watchmaker to be cleaned. Lord Randolph was annoyed, and told Winston he had better buy a cheap watch, as he was plainly unfit to take care of a good one. Lady Churchill, soothingly, sent Winston £2 and wrote wryly: 'Oh, Winny, what a harum scarum fellow you are!' Poor Winston: it had cost him (as he pointed out) £3 to hire the soldiers to drain the pond.

LIFE AT SANDHURST
The Royal Military College, Sandhurst, was founded in 1802. In the 1890s some 120 cadets entered the college every half year; a course lasted 16 months. Winston learned about guns, bridges, mapping, drill, how to keep regimental accounts and inspect meat! Army life made him punctual, or even early for classes.

Winston Graduates

Winston's father was determined he should enter a good infantry regiment; Winston was equally determined to become a cavalry officer, so that he could spend his time horse-riding. Otherwise army life would be dull: Britain had been at peace, at least in Europe, for 40 years. Winston turned for help to a family friend, Colonel Brabazon, who commanded the 4th Hussars. After visiting Brabazon at Aldershot, he wrote to tell Lord Randolph what an immensely smart regiment the Hussars were.

However, Lord Randolph was by now too ill to take a serious interest in Winston's career. He made a last effort to regain his health, by means of a round-the-world trip with Lady Churchill. While they were away, Winston completed his course at Sandhurst, graduating 20th in a class of 130.

Winston Defends the Music-Hall

Winston was now a young man-about-town. With cadet friends, he visited London at weekends. He enjoyed the Empire Theatre music-hall and made his first public speech, 'against the tyranny of prudes', after a minor riot involving students and 'do-gooders' who wished to curb the music-halls (which they thought were dens of vice where young men fell into bad company). Winston enjoyed the occasion, and looked forward to speaking at the side of his distinguished father. But this was not to be.

The Death of Lord Randolph

Lord Randolph returned home on Christmas Eve, 1894. He was beyond medical help, and on 24 January 1895 he died. (Seventy years later to the day, Winston himself was to die.)

Randolph's death removed the obstacle to Winston joining the 4th Hussars. At Aldershot there was riding practically all day. Winston was in his element, steeplechasing, fox hunting and playing polo.

In July 1895 came further sadness with the death (from peritonitis) of Mrs Everest. After being dismissed from the Churchill household, she had returned to a former employer, the Archdeacon of Barrow. Winston hurried to see her in London on learning of her illness, and hired a nurse to look after her. Her death took from him the person he had loved most, next to his mother. 'I shall never know such a friend again,' he wrote sadly.

Polo was the favourite game of young cavalry officers. Winston thought polo the finest game in the world and he became an enthusiastic member of his regimental team. Later, while serving in India, he travelled all over the country to play polo and spent much of his money on polo ponies.

In and Out of the Army

As head of the family, aware of his mother's extravagances and his own shaky finances, Winston now set about the urgent task of building a career. The army would not satisfy his ambitions.

The 4th Hussars were shortly to embark for service in India. During his leave, Winston visited the United States. He enjoyed New York, though he disliked American paper money (he preferred gold coins). He managed, through influential friends, to obtain permission to visit Cuba – then ruled by Spain and in the throes of a revolution. He saw fighting at first hand and earned some welcome fees for newspaper despatches, written for the London *Daily Graphic*.

In Cuba, Winston was allowed to accompany the Spanish troops of General Valdez fighting Cuban rebels. On his 21st birthday the young war correspondent came under fire for the first time.

India, and a Political Baptism

In London, Winston was introduced to important people: the banker Lord Rothschild, the politicians Asquith, Balfour and Chamberlain. But in September 1896 the army took him away, to India. India seemed dull, save for playing polo. Winston joined an expedition to the North-West Frontier in search of adventure, hoping to demonstrate his own courage by gaining a medal.

Instead, he wrote a book about the expedition, and it proved equally useful, for it caught the eye of the prime minister, Lord Salisbury. Winston needed influential people on his side, if he was to rise as swiftly as he planned.

While on leave in England, Winston made his first public speech at an election meeting near Bath. It was generally well received: one newspaper commented that 'he seems to be a young man of some ability, anxious to take a part in public affairs'. He was not yet 23 years old.

While on leave from army service in India, Winston made his first public speech from a political platform. Addressing a Primrose League meeting (supporting the Conservative party), he made a vigorous speech that in the words of one reporter 'delighted his audience'. The date was 26 July 1897, the place Claverton Manor near Bath, in Somerset.

THE SUDANESE WAR
In the Sudan, British and Egyptian forces fought the followers of the Muslim leader, the Mahdi Muhammad Ahmed and his successor, the Khalifa Abdullahi. The Mahdi's forces captured Khartoum, and killed General Gordon, in 1885. But General Kitchener's victory in 1898 at Omdurman finally defeated the rebels.

Ambitious for a Reputation

With the help of influential friends (including the prime minister) Winston got himself transferred to the 21st Lancers serving under General Kitchener in the Sudan. There he took part in a tailpiece of British military history: the cavalry charge at the battle of Omdurman. 'It passed like a dream', he wrote, recalling the thrilling charge. He was unscathed, after passing through 'the most dangerous two minutes I shall live to see'.

After this adventure, Winston turned his back on army life. In 1899 he resigned his commission, and stood for Parliament in a by-election at Oldham. He lost, but learned much about the business of fighting election battles.

The charge of the 21st Lancers at the battle of Omdurman, 2 September 1898. Of 310 Lancers who rode into the enemy lines, 21 were killed and 49 wounded. Winston was proud to have ridden in the British Army's last full-scale cavalry charge, though the Lancers' ride did not greatly influence the British victory. Kitchener's army defeated the Dervishes because it had more rifles and machine-guns.

A Prisoner of the Boers

The fame Winston sought came about shortly afterwards. He was now establishing himself as a writer and went to South Africa to report for the *Morning Post* on the war against the Boers. He was soon in the thick of it. Helping to rescue a train ambushed by Boer guerrillas, he was taken prisoner, after showing great bravery under fire.

News of the capture of Lord Randolph Churchill's son made headlines all around the world. Even greater was the sensation when, a few days later, Winston escaped! He climbed out of a lavatory window in the school where he and other British prisoners were being held and made his way to a mine manager's house. Fortunately, it was the one house in the vicinity owned by British people. Winston was hidden in a mine (in a stable used by pit-ponies) and later smuggled on to a train going to Portuguese East Africa.

He spent Christmas 1899 in Durban, a hero. Not even the shock of hearing that his brother Jack had been wounded by a Boer bullet could dim his satisfaction. He was famous. He would surely soon be in Parliament.

27

From MP to PM

Winston Churchill's long and distinguished parliamentary career began in October 1900, with his election as Member of Parliament for Oldham in Lancashire. He took his seat in the House of Commons, and at once felt at home in the place where his father had been such a prominent figure.

In 1904, however, he disagreed with Conservative policy on free trade and 'crossed the floor' to join the Liberal party. By 1906 he was a member of the Liberal government, and rose swiftly to high office.

An Ideal Marriage

On 12 September 1908 Winston was married in St Margaret's, Westminster (the parish church of the House of Commons). His bride was Clementine Hozier and, like him, she had had a rather unhappy childhood. Their marriage was to last for 57 years: Winston was to be grateful for his wife's support in the times of crisis they were to share.

Wartime Experience

In 1910 Churchill was home secretary; in 1911 he was first lord of the admiralty, strengthening Britain's navy in readiness for war.

During the First World War (1914-18) he worked strenuously for victory. He now knew 'what vile and wicked folly' war was, especially after the disasters at Gallipoli and the Dardanelles, military failures that damaged his career.

The First World War left Europe weakened and shocked. Millions had died, and people vowed that there must be no more war. The rise to power of Adolf Hitler in Germany, and of Japan in the East, brought the threat of a new war. Churchill was one of the few who warned of the danger.

Winston and Clementine shared many moments of joy and anxiety during their marriage. She checked his extravagances, warning him against the dangers of gambling, for example! Their family home, Chartwell in Kent, became a sanctuary from the cares of politics and war.

The Ins and Outs of Office

In the 1920s Churchill rejoined the Conservative party. He again held important office, as chancellor of the exchequer (in charge of national finances). But from 1929 to 1939 he was without a position, a lone voice in the political wilderness. He predicted war with Hitler's Nazi Germany and warned of Britain's weakness in the face of German rearmament. He wrote books, painted pictures, made speeches – and fretted at his 'lost years'.

The War Leader

When the Second World War began, in September 1939, Churchill was recalled to the government, to the admiralty. In May 1940 Britain turned to him to take over from Neville Chamberlain as prime minister. His moment had come.

From 1940 to 1945 Churchill symbolised Britain's wartime defiance. His cigar and 'V for Victory' sign became familiar to everyone. He worked tirelessly, meeting other allied leaders, visiting troops, planning new campaigns from the government headquarters in London.

During the Second World War Churchill's magnificent speeches inspired listeners and defied the Nazis: 'We shall fight on the beaches, we shall fight on the landing-grounds, we shall fight in the fields and in the streets, we shall fight in the hills. We shall NEVER surrender'.

The Great Commoner

On 8 May 1945 Churchill led Britain's celebrations of victory in Europe. Yet in July he was no longer prime minister. The British people had elected a Labour government, and the war leader's task was done.

In peacetime, Churchill warned of the threat of Communism bringing down the so-called 'iron curtain' across Europe. He received many honours, including a Nobel Prize. In 1951 he returned as prime minister, resigning in 1955. He was knighted in 1953 but refused any higher honour, preferring to remain in his beloved House of Commons.

On 24 January 1965, the 'great commoner' died. After an impressive state funeral ceremony in London, Sir Winston Churchill was laid to rest in Bladon churchyard, beside his parents and brother. He had become a part of the history he loved.

The Allied war leaders: Churchill, President Franklin D. Roosevelt of the USA, and Soviet leader Josef Stalin. The 'Big Three' met at Tehran in 1943 and at Yalta in 1945 to plan the final defeat of Germany and Japan. These meetings shaped the post-war world, particularly the division of Germany and the reorganization of much of Europe.

Important Events in Winston Churchill's Life

1874 Born at Blenheim Palace on 30 November
1882 School, at Ascot, Hove and finally Harrow
1893 Enters Royal Military College, Sandhurst
1895 Deaths of Randolph Churchill and Mrs Everest.
     Joins 4th Hussars
1896 Sails with his regiment to India; sees action on the North-West Frontier
1898 Rides in cavalry charge at battle of Omdurman
1899 Loses first election, at Oldham. Escapes from captivity in South Africa
1900 Enters Parliament as Conservative MP for Oldham
1904 Joins Liberal party
1908 Becomes president of board of trade. Marries Clementine Hozier
1910 Home secretary; sends troops against South Wales miners; rebuked by prime minister for recklessly risking his life at the siege of Sidney Street in London
1911 First lord of the admiralty
1914 First World War begins
1915 Loses admiralty job; resigns from government; joins army fighting in France
1917 Back in government, under prime minister David Lloyd George
1922 Out of Parliament until elected MP for Epping. Buys country house, Chartwell, which becomes family home

1924 Chancellor of exchequer in Stanley Baldwin's government
1929 Out of office
1933 Warns of dangers of war after Hitler comes to power in Germany
1936 Tries to prevent abdication of King Edward VIII
1939 Recalled to government as Second World War begins
1940 Succeeds Neville Chamberlain as prime minister
1941 USSR and United States enter war
1945 Allied victory; defeated in British general election, though he retains his seat as MP for Woodford
1951 Returns to power as prime minister in Conservative government
1953 Awarded Nobel Prize for Literature (his books include an autobiography *My Early Life*, a life of Marlborough, and *A History of the English-Speaking Peoples*). Knighted by young Queen Elizabeth II
1955 Resigns as prime minister and is succeeded by Anthony Eden
1963 Made honorary citizen of United States of America by President John F. Kennedy
1964 Retires as an MP with 'the unbounded admiration and gratitude of the House of Commons'
1965 Dies, on 24 January

Index